The Life-Changing Power of Gratitude

7 Simple Exercises that will Change Your Life for the Better

Includes a 3 Month Gratitude Journal

Marc Reklau

Disclaimer

This book is designed to provide information and motivation to our readers. It is
sold with the understanding that the publisher is not engaged to render any type of
psychological, legal, or any other kind of professional advice. The instructions and
advice in this book are not intended as a substitute for counseling. The content of
each chapter is the sole expression and opinion of its author. No warranties or
guarantees are expressed or implied by the author's and publisher's choice to
include any of the content in this volume. Neither the publisher nor the individual
author shall be liable for any physical, psychological, emotional, financial, or
commercial damages, including, but not limited to, special, incidental, consequential
or other damages. Our views and rights are the same:

You must test everything for yourself according to your own situation talents and
aspirations

You are responsible for your own decisions, choices, actions, and results.

Marc Reklau

Visit my website at www.marcreklau.com

ISBN-13: 9781790504251

"Gratitude makes sense of our past, brings peace for today, and creates a vision for tomorrow."

Melody Beattie

Contents

Acknowledgments

Writing the acknowledgments in a book is the most challenging part. Hardly nobody reads them, but if you forget somebody that feels they should be mentioned you are in trouble. I was very tempted just to leave them out, but of course when - if not in a book about gratitude is the time to remember all the people I'm grateful for to have, to have had or to have met in my life. I'll try to make this short.

First on the list is family: my mother Heidi and my Grandmother Hilde. Natalia, my partner in life and business. My father (R.I.P.),
My cousin Alexander, his wife, Yvonne, and Lola. Marc & Paula.
My old friends from all the soccer teams I played for. I can't name you all (no space), but you know who you are. Above all "Mein Entdecker" and substitute father Vlado Tumbas - the first coach to recognize my (hidden) talent as a soccer player.

My ex-colleagues and bosses. I also can't name you all, but I'm thinking of you while writing this.
My friends Pol, Imna, Albert Aderiu, Stefan Ludwig & family, Claudio & Anne-Sophie, Thomas Schmückle, Ralf "the Schwob" Pfeufer, Albert Wiethoff, Daniel "Klinsi" Doernen, Richard "Webesy" Weber, John Crescenzi, Jay Parkinson and all my other friends I met during my year at Disney. Not to forget the Henke family in Fort Lauderdale and my best friend from university Jorge Caro (if you read 30 DAYS you know him. He's the guy who always got laughing attacks when I wanted to throw in the towel)

Last but not least, thanks to everybody I met along the way. You were either a friend or a teacher, or both!

P.S. If I forgot you, please don't be mad and just write me an email to remember you when I write the acknowledgments for my next book.

Introduction

If you have read other books of mine, listened to an interview, saw me speak, or saw me on TV, then you know that I'm a huge fan and advocate of the power of gratitude. When I get asked what the secret of my success is, why things are working so well, or how I went from selling eight books a month to one thousand books a month, I usually answer that the main reason for great things happening in my life right now is almost probably the "Power of Gratitude," meaning the constant state of gratitude I'm in.

I'm grateful for the good things that happen every day and even for the good things that are on the way to me but not in my life yet. I'm grateful for every experience and grateful to be alive and healthy. There are so many reasons to be grateful. Unfortunately, many of us forget about them because we are so busy doing other things all the time.

Gratitude is one of the most powerful forces in the universe, and being grateful not only brings good things into our lives but also makes us notice more and more of those things that are already there. And when I talk about practicing gratitude, I don't talk about practicing it once a year or every now and then. I talk about practicing it every single day and throughout each day. Make gratitude a lifestyle.

In the last three years, my life has changed completely. I went from jobless to an international bestselling author. I left behind a marriage that had become toxic, and I am now in a good and healthy relationship. There are days when I earn in a day what I once made in a month and sometimes even more.

Why am I telling you all this in a book about gratitude? Because after a lot of thinking and reflecting, I came to the conclusion that the main factor for the amazing changes in my life—and one of the primary ingredients for my success—is gratitude. Of all the changes I made, the single biggest thing that I did was start to practice extreme gratitude. I remember the date when it happened. (Easy! It's on page one of my first gratitude journal.) I started writing down three things I was grateful for on November 11, 2013. It was these little things that came to my mind:

- I'm grateful that I'm alive.
- I'm grateful for my family.
- I'm grateful for my friends who support me.
- I'm grateful for the cup of coffee I had on the beach.
- I'm grateful for working hard.
- I'm grateful for that good lunch that I had with a friend.
- I'm grateful for that good presentation I attended.
- I'm grateful for a sunny day.

Okay, that's more than three …

The more grateful I became in my life—without expecting anything in exchange—the better and more successful my life became.

At the end of February 2015, I took gratitude to another level. That's when it all began to happen. In my eyes, it's not a coincidence that on March 31, 2015, my book *30 DAYS: Change Your Habits, Change Your Life* was downloaded close to 40,000 times in just a couple of days. That's when everything started to change.

Be grateful every day. Imagine what would happen if you were not only thankful once a year but every day.

When I prayed as a kid, giving thanks was a rather small part of my prayers. The bigger part was always asking, asking, asking. Give me this, give me that. And when I was giving thanks, it didn't come from my heart. I didn't feel it. I'll repeat it: gratitude works best when it comes from the heart and you feel the gratitude with every cell of your body.

You can really count on the universe, God, or whatever you believe in once you put gratitude in play. Then there will be more things to come that you can be grateful for. It seems to be a universal law. Gratitude really changes everything. Once you seriously start practicing gratitude, you'll see your world in an entirely different way, and everything will begin to change.

When you are grateful, this universal energy responds by giving you more things to be grateful for. Call it focus, call it energy. I can't fully explain how it works, but does it work! I also can't explain electricity, but if I flick a switch, my house has light, it is warm (or cool), and I can cook great meals.

When I switch gratitude on, amazing things happen in my life.

If you are grateful, it seems that God, life, the universe, or destiny says, "Look at you! You're happy with everything you have in your life. Let's give you more."

So be grateful for your parents, your friends, your health. To appreciate also means to grow. When you appreciate things, they grow. Appreciate every breath, appreciate every flower, enjoy your friends' company more. When you appreciate the good in your life, the good grows.

Unfortunately, the opposite is also true. Take a look at every word you say and everything you do. Are you speaking and acting from a spirit of gratitude? If so, then great things will come your way.

Remember, it's all a matter of practice, so give yourself time.

Don't be too demanding, and above all, don't beat yourself up if you don't see results right away. You will notice without fail that the more gratitude you irradiate, the more great people and things you will "attract." I write "attract" like this with quotation marks because I'm still not clear if we are really attracting them (Law of Attraction) or if we just see more of them and more of the good because we focus on it (Selective Perception). But hey, the result is the same, and that's the important thing.

Anyways what I wanted to say was that it seems that the more grateful we are, the more good things we attract to us. Being always on the run makes us miss the beauty that's all around us. That's why we take things for granted and don't take the time to appreciate things anymore. Stop, reflect, and remember that you have a lot of things to be grateful for.

And you know what is the best? Gratitude is the best antidote to all the negative emotions. Why? Because you can't feel negative emotions while you practice gratitude. You can't feel any kind of worry, anger, or depression while you practice gratitude. You can't even get upset about your current life circumstances while you're practicing gratitude. You can't be grateful and unhappy at the same time. You can't be grateful and worried at the same time. You can't be grateful and angry at the same time. Shall I go on?

So why is it so friggin' challenging to be grateful? To be honest, it's not difficult at all. All you have to do is to write down three things you are grateful for every day for the next six to eight weeks, and your life will change for the better. If you take my word for it and start doing it right now, you don't even have to read this book. Really. Just do it! The results will be awesome. And not because I say so or because Oprah says so or because it's in the Bible or because self-help gurus say so. No. It's because science proves it.

Prosperity is often just around the corner. Many people are practicing the principles and habits of success but stay stuck or poor.

Something is blocking them from success. It could be a lack of forgiveness, but the only reason for it is often a lack of gratitude.

If gratitude came in pill form, it would fly off the shelves. It's easy but not that easy. You still have to do a little work. Five minutes a day should do it.

I'd be happy if you joined me on this gratitude journey through this book. I have some fantastic studies and stories lined up for you.
Let's dive in

CHAPTER ONE
The Power of Gratitude

Why is it so difficult to be grateful? Why do things always have to get really bad before we appreciate what we have? Why can't we appreciate people in our lives until they're gone? Why did I take forty years to adopt the attitude of gratitude?

Personally, I don't know. It was right in front of my nose all along, but I just couldn't wrap my mind around being grateful for what I had or, even less, something I didn't have yet. Even worse, I took things for granted or felt entitled. And those two states are the archenemies of gratitude and lead us directly to an unsatisfying life or even worse—depression.

Look at it closely. If you felt grateful for your job, would you hate it? Would you complain about getting up and going to work? I think not.

When do relationships get worse? That's right. When we take them for granted, when we don't appreciate our partners anymore. (Yes. I'm guilty of doing that more than once.)

It doesn't have to be that way if we learn to adopt an attitude of gratitude as a way of life. It will take our lives to the next level, and yes, there is always something to be grateful for. Even cancer and AIDS patients found reasons to be grateful, and when terminally-ill patients were interviewed, they said things like, "For the first time in my life, I feel like I'm alive," or "For the first time in my life, I appreciate ..."

A lot of the time, we don't show or express enough gratitude in our lives, but like everything, it can be practiced. When we express gratitude over and over again, it becomes a habit, and it changes everything in our lives. We enjoy life more, we get more resilient, we see more opportunities, we become more social, and a lot more.

In a study conducted by Robert Emmons and Michael McCullough from UC Davis, people who wrote down five things they were grateful for every night before going to bed were more optimistic, happier, healthier, more generous, more benevolent, and much more likely to achieve their goals than people who didn't write anything down, wrote down five hassles, or wrote down five things they were better at than others.

Gratitude recharges you with energy, boosts your self-worth, and is directly linked to physical and mental well-being. It leads you directly to happiness, and as I mentioned before, it's the best antidote to anger, envy, and resentment.

Start the day by saying thank you for what you have instead of complaining about what you don't have or listing all the things you fear or hate about the coming day—which is actually the complete opposite of gratitude. Doing so will have an immediate effect on your life. Focus on the good things that you can find every day.

I know. It's easy to be grateful when things are going well, so it's always better to start with gratitude when things are going well. Nevertheless, I have had countless clients who were in a bad place when they started with gratitude.

Of course, it's a lot more difficult when you are in a bad place, when you are suffering, when you are sad, when one disappointment follows another, when things don't seem to work out, when you are totally stressed, and when life is not going so great. It's also most important to be grateful for these situations, and believe me, there is always something to be grateful for. Start with the most essential things: you are breathing, you are alive, and there is somebody who cares for you. Start there. You'd be surprised by how long the list can become.

Start with what you have.

1. You are alive—today and any day there are millions of people who don't wake up from their sleep.
2. You are breathing (see number one.)
3. You have a roof over your head.
4. You have a caring family.
5. You have food on the table.

Oh, look. That's already five things, and I told you that you can start with only three things!

Never, ever, *ever* get caught up in the vicious cycle of "I'll be grateful when I get a new job," "when the kids go to school," "when I lose some weight," "when I win the lottery." When, when, when! That is not gratitude. That is the opposite of gratitude, and you might even "attract" more bad things into your life.

One of the big problems is that while we wait for things to happen that we could be grateful for and focus on them, we forget to see everything we already have in our lives to be grateful for. It's when we start focusing on everything that we can be grateful for right now that everything will begin to happen.

So let's start right here! What can you be grateful for?
We already said it: you are *alive*, and you are reading this book. That means you woke up this morning while many other people on this planet didn't. You are breathing. Phew! Yes, you can already start being grateful.

Why are we always taking *life* for granted? We live like we would live eternally, leaving happiness and other important things for later. Every now and then, we get a reminder— somebody close to us gets sick or even dies. Then we stop and reflect for a moment and promise to live more mindfully until a couple of days later, we fall back into our same old bad habits.

Stop for a second now. I mean right now. Be grateful for the gift of being life and being able to breathe. Let it become part of your nature! Be grateful for what you have, for all the small things around you, and even for the things you don't have yet.

Wow! Did that feel great? Can we agree that no matter at what point you are right now, you can be grateful to be alive and kicking (or better-said, breathing)? Yes? Great! It's a start.

CHAPTER TWO
Let's get started

The power of gratitude can change your life beyond belief. But before that, you need to have a look where you are right now. What do you have right now to be grateful for and, more importantly, in which parts of your life are you not feeling grateful?

Where are you not feeling grateful? In which areas of your life to you take things for granted? Where do you feel entitled?

A quick warning: feeling entitled to something is the fastest road to unhappiness, frustration, or even depression. I'm sorry that I have to be the one who tells you that life doesn't owe you anything. Society doesn't owe you anything. God doesn't owe you anything. In short, *nobody owes you anything*. That might be a tough pill to swallow at first, but I might have done you the biggest favor of your life. Once you stop feeling entitled, you can start taking responsibility and just go and get what you want. It might not be easy, it might cost you effort and work, but you will be able to get it.

So let's get back to the original question of this book. What can you be grateful for? Write it here:

I'm grateful for _____

Let's dig a bit deeper. What could you be thankful for but aren't? Write it here:

I could be thankful for _____, but until now, I took it for granted. From today on I'll be grateful for it.

Ok. After this short introduction, it's time to get working. The two exercises I recommend to all my readers of all my books, all my coaching clients, all the participants in my workshops, all the attendees at my conferences, and all the people at my company consulting are the following:

1. Make a list of all the things you are grateful for. This should be a long list, and you should add to this list every day.
2. Write down three to five things that you are grateful for every day.

Start working right away. You don't need to finish reading this book to start making the lists.

Here's how you go about it. Let's start with number one: your list of things you can be grateful for. Take a notepad or a journal and start writing. Here are some prompts:

- How are your finances? Do you have savings? Is your money well managed?
- How are things at work? Do you still enjoy your job? Are you grateful to have one?
- How are your social life and love life going? Are you loved and accepted by your friends and family? Do you have a great partner and great friends?
- Do you have goals in your life? Do you know where you are going? Are you on your way to reaching your goals?
- How do you feel about your body? Are you healthy? What parts are going well? What isn't working so well.
- Do you have a lot of energy? Are you eating well? Are you able to shop for great food?
- How is your home? Are you happy with where you live? Do you like what you have or do you want more? What are you longing for?

You know what? Make a second list! Separate from the list where you wrote everything that you are grateful for, make a list of everything that you *should* be grateful for but you're not (no judging or beating up yourself here. Just make the list)

Once you have your two lists, we're going to figure it out. Ready? Okay!

Now, look at your second list. Do you already notice what you could be more grateful for? Careful. No self-blaming and self-torturing here. There's no problem. You are becoming aware. So look at your second list and change your perspective.

Once you start looking at things differently, the things you look at change! Start to change your way of looking at things, your way of thinking, and suddenly you have even more to feel grateful for. This will change your life forever.

Read your gratitude list right after waking up. If you read this list once a day and add to it frequently, the gratitude effect gets bigger and bigger. Try it. It can make a lot of difference. Imagine how your days would start if you read your gratitude list first thing in the morning. And as they say, the start of the day determines how the rest of the day goes.

It's so powerful because instead of waking up unfocused, worried or even dreading what's going to come today from the second you wake up, you'll get an energy boost from your gratitude list, which shows you all the things you can be grateful for already. By writing it down and adding to it, you are imprinting yourself with gratitude, and every morning when you read your list, this feeling will get stronger and stronger.

By reviewing the list day after day, you will slowly memorize it without even realizing it. After a while, just looking at the list will trigger the feeling of gratitude within you. That's why this list is so important. You can use the list any time during the day to give yourself a quick thirty-second boost of gratitude.

Remember, don't say, "I'll be grateful when ..." as I did for many years. Take the shortcut. Be grateful *now* no matter what and make gratitude a daily habit. Start the day by saying thank you for what you have instead of complaining about what you don't have. This will have an immediate effect on your life. Focus on the good things that you can find every day.

The "Attitude of Gratitude" has gone from being a purely spiritual thought, something you could believe or not believe, something you could try or not to a scientifically proven process to improve our lives. We owe this to people like Dr. Robert Emmons, who studied the countless benefits of gratitude and proved them scientifically. This robs us of any excuse not make gratitude a part of our life.

To reap this benefits, start now with the second exercise. Write down three to five things you are grateful for every day. You can do it in the morning or in the evening or, if you want to have a double dose of happiness, in the morning *and* the evening. Before going to sleep, relive the moments. Relive the happiness. It's important to *feel* the happiness and the state of gratitude.

Don't worry if it's a bit difficult to find three things you are grateful for at the beginning. You are training your mind. Give it some time. It will get better and better. This will work. As I mentioned before, it's scientifically proven that if you are grateful for just five minutes a day, you feel considerably happier after just three to four weeks!

Here are some more tips on how to get the most out of the second exercise:

- Do it consistently without fail (unfortunately, that's what most people don't manage to do).
- Don't give up if you don't see immediate results.
- **Feel** the gratitude! Don't just repeat things that you think you "should" be grateful for and not really feel that feeling of gratitude resonating inside you. You need to feel the gratitude.

Gratitude works for everybody. In the last five years I've been studying and practicing it, I've seen only two cases where it didn't work.

In the first case, it's when you say, "At least I have this, at least I have that ..." That's not gratitude. That's coming from a place of lacking. And what happens when you're focusing on what you're lacking? You see ("attract") *more* lackings!

In the second case, it's when you are so stuck in your hectic workday and routine or—even worse—a negative mindset that you think it's just impossible to come up with something you are grateful for. Here are a few examples:

- Stress, fear, doubt, and worry control your life, and you can't for even a moment calm your mind and think of anything that you could be grateful for.
- You try to be grateful, but all that you can think of is everything you don't have and all the things that are going wrong. (Be about careful what you focus on. You'll only get more of it.)
- As soon as you try to come up with something you could be grateful for, the voice in your head says, "You have **nothing** to be grateful for! Life is just a big, continuous struggle."
- You think, "Today is not a great day for that gratitude thing. Maybe tomorrow something great will happen that I can be really grateful for. I'll start tomorrow."
- It seems that this whole law of attraction nonsense doesn't work for you because you keep on attracting what you don't want instead of what you do want.

Does any of this sound familiar to you? Here's what you can do:

1. Ask yourself, **"If I had something to *feel* grateful for, what would it be?"**

2. Look back at your life and think of all the things you could be grateful for even though they are not a part of your daily life anymore. We often forget to be grateful when things changed for the better. You can be grateful for that now.
3. Think of a time in the past when things weren't going so well but eventually turned out fine. Wouldn't you have been immensely grateful for that back then? It's never too late to show gratitude.
4. If a friend asked you, "What should I be grateful for?" what answer would you give them?
5. If you still can't come up with anything to be grateful for, try some (actually, all) of these things you could be grateful for:
   o Yourself
   o Being alive
   o Three meals a day
   o Being healthy
   o Your body
   o Your friends and family
   o Your talents
   o Your achievements
   o The place you live
   o Nature
   o Business partners
   o Random acts of kindness
   o Painful lessons that you overcame
   o The power of hope

There is a lot to be grateful for. Look within, and you'll undoubtedly find a long list

Action Steps

1.Make a list of everything you have in your life that you are grateful for. Write down everything you can think of (this should be a long list).

2.Make a list of everything you should be grateful for but aren't and meditate on it. Change your perspective (no self-torturing allowed).

3.Write down three to five things that you are grateful for that day in your journal. Before going to sleep, relive the moments. Relive the happiness.

Remember: It's crucial to *feel* the happiness and the state of gratitude and not to go through the motions mechanically. Feel the gratitude with your whole body. Visualize and make it as real as you can. If you do the exercise in the morning just after waking up and at night before going to sleep, it will be even more powerful!

One last note. Tal Ben Shahar mentions that it's better to do this exercise of gratitude once a week *mindfully* than to do it every day without caring for it. The important thing is the intensity of the emotion.

I still recommend that you do it every day with lots of emotion.

CHAPTER THREE
The Impact of Gratitude on Your Social Relationships

Say Thank You!

Gratitude improves not only your health and mindset but also your relationships (which, by the way, are the number one predictor of your future happiness and success). It's not enough to feel grateful and appreciative towards people and staying silent. You must *show* this gratitude and appreciation to everybody who deserves it.

Saying "please" and "thank you" goes a long way, today more than ever because it seems that these kind of manners are not *en vogue* anymore.

It's human nature to like and respond to people who appreciate us and show gratitude. Be grateful to people and show it to them with kind words or little gestures, and you can rest assured that it will come back to you multiplied. Showing gratitude is a way of showing people that you respect them.

When was the last time someone said thank you to you, and you knew they meant it? Wasn't it magical? Start thanking people around you for doing their job, for being kind, for doing favors.

Being grateful is as great for you as the person you are grateful to. It makes everything work better, and it's a real joy to be around grateful people. It's worth a try, isn't it? But there are some ground rules to follow:

1. You have to be sincere and really mean it when you thank people. People can distinguish very well if you are genuinely thankful or not. If it's not real, you'll reap none of the

benefits. Say "Thank you," "I appreciate you," or "I am glad to have you in my life" loudly and clearly. Say it with joy. Maintain eye contact. It means a lot more when you look the people you thank in the eyes. Say, "Thank you, Peter," "Thank you, Mary."

2. Use people's names. It makes a huge difference.
3. Practice thanking people. It will change your life. If you want to become a master at thanking people, thank them for not only the obvious but also the not so obvious.

It's so simple and yet so powerful. Few things are more important than the ability to properly thank people.

Have you noticed that if you thank people for some well-done work, they often want to give you more? They know that if they give you more, they will probably be rewarded again.

Smile

Smiling at people goes a long way, and it's an effortless way to say thank you. When you smile, your entire body sends out the message "life is great" to the world.

Smiling is also contagious. Try it! Smile at someone, and in most cases, they will smile back and be helpful to you. With a smile, you can make most people friendly and cooperative within seconds.

Keeping in mind that people subconsciously decide if they like us or not in a couple of seconds, that those first few seconds decide in which direction the relationship goes, and that this direction is complicated to change afterward, make sure to meet people with your most sincere smile. It will do miracles. Your chances of getting the date or getting the job will skyrocket. As the cheesy saying goes, "You never get a second chance to make a first impression."

Smile at the baker, the butcher, at people in the subway, and at the employee at the newspaper stand, and see what happens. Smile even when you are talking on the phone! The person on the other end of the phone will notice it. Nobody can resist against sincere politeness, a good heart, and a smile.

One last thing: smiling is good for not only your relationships but also your health. Smiling a lot every day improves your mental state. Have you ever tried being a pessimist while smiling? It's difficult if not impossible to think unhappy thoughts while you are smiling because the physical act of smiling changes your inner chemistry and alters your stress response in challenging situations.

Smiling not only improves your creativity but also sends a signal to your brain that everything is all right. If you smile, you will be perceived as more confident, and people will be more likely to trust you. Heck, people just feel good around you!

Action Steps

1. Make a list of all the people around you. When is the last time you were grateful for them being in your life? When was the last time you said thank you to them?
2. Say thank you and mean it. Be honest.

How does this make you feel? Do this every day from now on.

CHAPTER FOUR
The Effect of Gratitude on Your Mind

Now that you have learned how gratitude improves your relationships, let's look at the things that are going well in our lives.

What are the things you have in your life that you take for granted? There are so many things, relationships, and friendships in our lives that we don't value until they are gone. We often take people who have a positive impact on us for granted without being aware of it. It's human. It happens to all of us; still, you'll be much better off becoming aware of these things, people, and special relationships *now* rather than when it's too late.

Sometimes it's difficult to grasp and quantify this, especially if you have a very stressful life or going through some hard times. I don't want to sound harsh, but those are the times when you have to make an even greater effort to appreciate everything you have.

If you have kids who love you, parents who are there for you, or friends who have your back, then when was the last time you were truly grateful that you had them? A long time ago? Put them on your gratitude list and include them when you write down the three to five things you are grateful for today.

Do you have a place of your own, a house, a car that drives you anywhere, excellent restaurants in the area, a great takeaway place? Yes, you can be grateful for those, too! There are so many things you can be grateful for if you stop taking things for granted! Find those things.

Let's dig a little deeper. Look around you. Can you see? Yes? That means you are not blind. You could be grateful for that. Can you distinguish colors? Well, that's another thing you can be grateful for.

It's all a matter of perspective, just like Hellen Keller once said, "I cried because I had no shoes until I met a man who had no feet."

Let's go (mentally) to your closet. Are there clothes in it? Yours? Bingo! Feel the gratitude for having clothes. I'm not kidding. At the end of this book, I want you to *feel* grateful for *everything*! It will be worth it.

Let's continue: Do you have shelter? Do you have a house or apartment that protects you from the sun, rain, and wind? And? Have you ever felt grateful for it? I hope so. If not, start now.

I think you've noticed it by now: You don't have to find huge things to be grateful for. You can start with small things, with things you already have and just took for granted until now. This is how the magic gets started. A little gratitude for small things here, a little gratitude for small things there, and you start reprogramming your mind to scan your world for positive stuff.

The great thing about our miraculous minds is that you see more of what you concentrate on (this is also called selective perception). The reticular activation system (RAS) determines the lenses through which you look at the world. If you look for things you can be grateful for, you'll see more things you can be grateful for, and they keep adding up! I'm getting excited just writing this!

If you make gratitude a habit, you will start to focus on what is positive and good in your life and world. The bad parts of your life won't magically disappear all of a sudden, but gratitude also makes you more resilient, which means you are better able to cope with the negative aspects of your life and you can recover faster from the low blows.

I had one client who we'll call Petra. When I started coaching her, she was in a tough place. Her relationship was not at its best, and she worked hard but didn't even have a salary—she only got a commission from sales. So apart from strategizing and tracing plans, we worked on gratitude, and she did the same thing I'm asking you to do. Petra wrote down three to five things she was grateful for every day.

After two weeks, Petra told me, "Marc, I don't know if I'm going crazy. Nothing has changed in my situation, but I'm just happier now."

We kept on working. After another four weeks, Petra had a working contract with exactly the minimum salary that she wanted. Six months later, she called me. She had turned her life around. Her relationship was going well, she had tripled her salary, and everything she touched turned to gold. It all started with gratitude!

It's scientifically proven that gratitude boosts our optimism and makes us see more opportunities. Success—however that might look to you—is just the logical consequence of our elevated optimism, better attitude, and cashing in on some of the opportunities that are all around us.

If you are a pessimist, you might need a bit more than gratitude alone to turn into an optimist, but it's a start. Science has proven that pessimism is not genetic and not a state that can't be changed. You can learn to become an optimist. Moving out of the negative thinking towards gratitude is a fantastic first step.

Remember that gratitude is the very best antidote to painful emotions—and a *choice.*

Yes. Sometimes, it's tough to find something to be grateful for. We just want to be sad and unhappy and dwell on our pain. But the moment you say enough is enough and start concentrating on things you can be grateful for, you start moving towards more happiness.

If you spend time being grateful every day, you will naturally become happier. That doesn't mean you'll be happy all the time—nobody is! That also wouldn't be normal. Ups and downs and painful emotions are an important part of life. What will happen, though, is that you'll recover more quickly from the downs and be able to enjoy the ups even more. When you have challenging circumstances, replace your thoughts with gratitude.

Further proven benefits of the "Attitude of Gratitude" are increased confidence, improved health, fewer headaches, better sleep, and an increased level of enjoying life experiences. What will happen to your life when you are grateful for everything and start acting from gratitude instead of defensiveness, mistrust, or negativity?

The best part is that all this becomes a self-fulfilling prophecy. You become happier and good things happen to you. Your confidence raises, and you become more optimistic and expect even more good things to happen to you, and then they do, which gives you more confidence and optimism, and then even more good things happen to you, and so on. Indeed, it's a virtuous circle and an upwards spiral.

Another positive side effect is that as you become happier you naturally "attract" people, things, and situations that make you happier and, thus, create a life that is beyond your wildest imagination. That's the power of gratitude, the most powerful force in the universe.

As I mentioned before, I started with gratitude in November 2013, roughly six weeks after being let go from my job. Today—not even five years later—I'm writing these lines on my fifty-foot yacht in a beautiful marina next to the Mediterranean Sea. My books have been read by over 200,000 readers, I'm speaking and training at companies, and I can earn in a day what before I made in a month.

I'm not telling you this to show off. I'm saying it to show what the power of gratitude can do for you, too. If I can do it, you can do it! I get mail almost daily with people telling me how much they improved thanks to the power of gratitude.

CHAPTER FIVE
The Attitude of Gratitude and Your Body

Gratitude makes everything better. Remember that doing the gratitude exercises for four to six weeks will automatically make you more optimistic. So what about your body? It's now scientifically proven that optimism and a positive attitude are good for your health!

When Glen Affleck studied people who had had a heart attack, he found out that people who saw the heart attack as a wakeup call, as a sign to take better care of themselves, as a sign to revise their lifestyle and their value were more likely to survive and less likely to have another heart attack.

Another study on AIDS patients revealed that those who found benefits in their situation, such as appreciating things more, focusing on the things that really matter, or getting closer to certain people, were more likely to survive.

The most famous study on the health benefits of optimism is the so-called Nun Study, which showed that joy prolongs our lives. In 1932, 178 nuns had to write biographical sketches of themselves. Scientists looked at various factors and found one predictor of longevity: positive feelings.

The nuns' writings were sorted into four categories: most positive, least positive, and two categories in between. And here comes the mind-boggling result: after eighty-five years, 90% of those in the most-positive category and only 34% of those in the least-positive category were alive. After ninety years, 54% of those in the most-positive category and only 11% of those in the least-positive category were still alive.

This doesn't mean that there weren't some pessimistic nuns who lived longer or that there weren't there some optimistic nuns who died earlier. But on an average, the optimists lived longer.

Apart from these scientifically proven facts, it's also a fact that when we feel good about ourselves, we take better care of ourselves. We eat healthier and probably even enjoy exercising or long walks, which in turn, makes us feel even happier. Another example of a virtuous circle. Today we can say it that without a doubt, a happy body is a healthy body.

Another side effect is that gratitude has a positive influence on your emotions, and that might cause you to refrain from binge eating or frustration eating, so you will not satisfy unsatisfied emotional needs with food.

If you are not very happy with your body right now, focus on what's working well. It's the same as always. Focus on what's working well, and there will be more parts working well soon. Focus on what you like about your body and continue doing your gratitude exercises. And remember, it's great to be alive and breathing. No matter how you are feeling, continue with gratitude and love and accept yourself just the way you are today.

CHAPTER SIX
Is it all good, even the bad stuff?

Um, the short answer is *yes*! I'm not kidding. Let me explain.

Bad things happen to good people. Period. Even when we are focusing on the good things most of the time, bad things are part of life, and sometimes shit happens. Shall we be grateful for that too? Well, yes. If possible. Perspective is everything, my friend, and I can vouch for the fact that there is something good in every bad if you just look for it hard enough. So if the famous "sh*t happens," use it as fertilizer.

Tell you to be grateful for the bad things that happen to you is not to say that what has happened is good. It's not about lying down and waiting for the next curveball life sends you. Being grateful even for the bad things that happen is a sign of extreme maturity. It's about learning. It's about growth.

I've seen a lot of very bad things in my life. The ability to learn from the bad things in life has saved me and has made me the person I am today. The ability to be deeply grateful for these experiences has multiplied everything in my life.

Don't get me wrong. I prefer the positive experiences a thousand times, but when the sh*t hits the fan, you can only become strong and get through the experience when you know that you will learn from it and one day in the future and might even be grateful that it happened because something good came out of it.

You can do it. People are doing it right now at this moment. If they can do it, you can do it. And you have an advantage. You know about the life-transforming power of gratitude!

When you look at the most successful people, their lives often weren't a walk in the park. Many times, their life stories are full of struggle, hurt, and even abuse. Somehow, they rose above it and kept on going. You can do so by seeing your situation as something that makes you grow, not as something that will break you. Again, this is not easy, and you need a lot of guts to make it, but you can make it. They made it. I made it. You can make it.

Don't worry. Being grateful for the bad things won't bring more bad things in your life. It will bring even more things to be grateful for into your life. Being grateful for the bad things is letting go. It's all about perspective.

I always remember the following story:

Once upon a time, there were twin brothers. Their father was an alcoholic who mistreated them and abused them psychologically. They had a horrible childhood. When they grew up, one brother turned out to become a successful businessman. He was the sweetest person, liked by everybody and always ready to give others a hand, donating to charity. The other brother became like his father. He was an alcoholic, a mean, abusive, miserable person who was a pain for everyone.

One day, the old family doctor came to see the businessman. He asked him, "How did you do it? How did you become so successful?"
The businessman said, "Doctor, you should know. You knew my father."

Then the doctor was called to the house of the other brother. It was a horrible place. You could feel the tension and bad vibes right away. The doctor asked the second twin, "How could it come so far? Why are you leading such a miserable life?"

The second twin answered, "Doctor, you should know. You knew my father."

Two people can have the exact same experience in life—bad things happening to good people. They can live through the same unfortunate events and yet deal with them in a completely different ways. The way they deal with the circumstances life throws at them makes all the difference. Be like the first twin!

You can become depressed and burdened by continually concentrating on the pain of past events (be careful what you focus on), or you can focus on gratitude—gratitude for being alive, for surviving, for not giving up, for growing, for learning your lessons from the curveballs life (or other people) have thrown at you.

It's all good, even the bad things, if *you* make it so, and I'm 100% convinced that you can. Remember, every day is a gift! Don't take it for granted.

Nietzsche said it, Kelly Clarkson sings it, science has proven it: "What doesn't kill us makes us stronger." This is a fact. It's a truth, but it only works if you choose the path of growth, gratitude, love, and forgiveness

Forgiveness is another huge thing. Being able to forgive someone for what they did isn't about if what they did was right or wrong. They don't even have to know that you have forgiven them. It's about what happens inside you during the process.

Why forgive someone who did you wrong? Well, it's a selfish act! You're doing it for yourself. Who has the sleepless nights? Who is full of anger? Who loses the magic of the present moment?

As you forgive people, situations, the universe, and even yourself, you get rid of a lot of negative power that these people and events have held over you, and you liberate a lot of energy. Anger, resentment, and even worse, reliving hate over and over again are huge energy drains.

Sometimes, the only thing that holds us back from success or riches is an energy block caused by not being able to forgive. Once the negative power is out of the way, you might even be able to be grateful for the person or the event. I'm deeply grateful for all the events and people who have hurt me—and there were a lot, believe you me. They helped me become the person I am today, and I'm mighty happy about that.

Just remember that forgiving doesn't mean you can't put limits on others' behavior or call them out on the spot. But when you do forgive, make sure to forgive and let go. Don't fall into the trap of thinking of what could have, should have, and would have been. This just leads to a massive sense of loss, hurt, and frustration. From this place, it's very difficult to let go and move on. Try to focus on how "the bad stuff" has shaped you, how it helped you become a better person, and how this will serve to help you make better decisions in the future.

Remember, success is the result of the right decisions, the right decisions are the result of experience, and experience is the result of the wrong decisions.

I know I'm repeating myself, but I can't say it enough: focus on the positive, and you'll see more positive. Focus on gratitude, and you *will* see things you can be grateful for even in some of the worst experiences. Give yourself time. Sometimes, it takes a while.

Don't use your scars as reminders of how bad it was. Use them as reminders of how you have survived, of the battles you have won, of the things you learned. The most painful lessons make us the wisest. You're still here. Keep on going and, above all, be grateful.

CHAPTER SEVEN
It's all good, even the bad stuff!

Many times, going through rough times make you stronger, and when things don't seem to work out, you sometimes end up being in the right place anyway.

Being grateful for even the bad experiences doesn't mean that you want more of them. It means that you are grateful for the personal growth that came from these experiences. You made it through. You're still alive. You beat them. You dealt with them. Woah, that feels good, doesn't it?

I've said it before, and I'm not getting tired of repeating it: learning from past experiences and wrong decisions means you don't need to repeat the lesson again. Did you ever notice that some mistakes or situations repeat until you learned from them? This might be the last thing you want to hear if you recently went through tough times, but bear with me. I've been there. Believe me.

Of course, we all need a bit of wound-licking time, a bit of self-pity every now and then. It's okay. It's human, and it's part of the healing process as long as we keep it in the right measure. Too much of it can quickly send us towards a downward spiral.

Don't let your life's experiences negatively control you. You are in charge. Really, you are. Somewhere in all the horribleness of the circumstances, there is something positive, there is something to be grateful for. Find it!

How many times did it happen to you that a big love ended? You thought it was the end of the world. You thought you'd never love again, and then sometime later, somebody even better came around.

My father's death was a horrible event. It could have easily broken me, but I decided that it wouldn't negatively affect me. On the contrary, I decided that it would only affect my life positively. And it did.

Today, I'm grateful that I learned the value of my life in my early adult years. It taught me to enjoy and be grateful for every minute of my life because we never know how long we have left on our beautiful planet Earth. It taught me to live responsibly and without regrets. It taught me that it is better to try and fail than to not even try.

Find something to be grateful for even in the direst circumstances and let go of the pain.

When you are in the middle of horrible experiences, you might feel hopeless and think, "What good will come from this situation?" Or you might wonder why some doors don't open, why you spend time with some people, why this, why that.

Trust in the words of Steve Jobs, who at his famous speech at Stanford said, "You can't connect the dots looking forward; you can only connect them looking backward. So you have to trust that the dots will somehow connect in your future. You have to trust in something—your gut, destiny, life, karma, whatever. This approach has never let me down, and it has made all the difference in my life."

Trust that one day you will look back and everything will make sense. You will see that these times were the very ones that shaped you, and you will sit back with a smile, acknowledging that it was all worthwhile.

Remember these words: always concentrate on the bigger picture. Sometimes, you can't see it right away. A year from now, you will look back on it, and everything will make sense.

I also thank God, the universe, life, destiny—whichever you prefer —that I was let go from my job five years ago. While I was jobless, I studied online marketing and self-publishing, wrote my book, and published it. Today, I'm living a life I never ever even dared to dream of. I fulfilled my childhood dream to live on a boat, I get paid to travel to speak in other countries, and more than 200,000 readers have read my books. Sometimes the most magnificent things can happen out of the worst situations, and the tough moments in our lives can often be a blessing in disguise.

Sometimes, tough things happen in life—maybe a loss, problems, pain, the death of a loved one. These things can break us or turn us into the person we need to become to reach our goals. It's all a matter of perspective and attitude, and gratitude will give us the power to make the right choices.

Learn your lessons, and get the best out of every experience. It's possible. The world is full of people who have overcome the most dire experiences to go on and become successful—or maybe they became successful because they defeated these circumstances and dealt with them the right way. You will never stop learning, and you will notice that overcoming hard times and obstacles gets easier with time.

The attitude of gratitude will help you become more resilient, overcome hard times, bounce back, and "attract" more experiences that you can be grateful for.

Don't give up. It's all good, even the bad things.

CHAPTER EIGHT
Things you can be Grateful For

Remember, practicing gratitude is like exercising. If we decide to start exercising, we accept that we'll need time to see results. We won't run a marathon after one week of practice, and we won't lose twenty pounds in one week. On the other hand, when it comes to the mind, we have less patience. We write down our affirmations for a week, and if the desired wish doesn't come into our life immediately, we give up and, even worse, think that "this stuff doesn't work."

I've been reading self-help books for nearly thirty years now. For twenty-five years, nothing happened. But in the last four years, when I started practicing, taking action, having patience, and sticking with the exercises for months, everything changed.

If you stick to this exercises for six weeks, you will see results. It's scientifically proven. It will work for you too. And then, my friend, I recommend you continue. This is not an every-once-in-a-while thing. This is a lifestyle. Make gratitude your lifestyle, and you may achieve things you never ever even dreamed of because that's what gratitude does!

By now, you have hopefully started your gratitude list and are making a list of all the things you can be grateful for. This list will help you on the not-so-great days. These will still come every now and then because they are part of life, but gratitude will help you recover faster.

You probably have already noticed that gratitude and being grateful becomes easier the more you practice it. Use this list as a starting point for all the things you can be grateful for. Use it as a little inspiration for your own list. Don't just copy it. Let it inspire you to come up with your own items. The list has to be *yours*. The gratitude has to be *yours* and come from inside of *you*—and don't forget to *feel* the gratitude.

I wrote my first gratitude list on August 17, 2013.
Let's go. You can be grateful for

- Being you
- Your life
- Being alive
- Being able to have three meals a day
- Being healthy
- Your body
- Your friends and family
- Your talents
- Your achievements
- Where you live
- Former places you have lived
- The climate
- The beach
- Nature
- Random acts of kindness
- Painful lessons that you overcame
- Good things that are going to come into your life
- The city you live in
- The country you live in
- Freedom
- Clean drinking water
- Learning opportunities
- Your parents and grandparents
- Special people in your life
- Having the support of your loved ones
- Yourself (Yup! That also counts)
- Having clothes that protect you
- Having shoes that protect your feet
- Having a means of transportation (car, bike, etc.)
- Public transportation)

- Having access to a computer
- Having an internet connection
- Your skills
- Your ability to connect with people
- Your job and former jobs
- Your teachers
- Your mentors
- Books
- CDs
- Learning programs
- Business partners
- Being able to practice your hobbies
- Your emotions
- Milestones in your life
- Your birthday
- Memories
- Holidays, field trips, cities you've visited
- Weekends at the beach or in the mountains
- Being able to feel
- Strangers smiling at you
- Pets
- Laughing
- Things that didn't work out
- Doors that didn't open (something better was waiting)
- Lessons learned
- Technical advancements (Yes you can be grateful for the internet, Amazon, video calls, etc.)

How about this as a starting point for your own list? Looking good?

Add to this list every day, and read it first thing in the morning after getting up. Can you imagine how different your days will be when your first thoughts in the morning are full of gratitude?

Remind yourself to be grateful throughout the day. Once it becomes second nature, incredible things will happen! If you want to multiply the effect, read the list again just before going to sleep.

CHAPTER NINE
Write in your journal

You're still here! That's great news! I see you are taking the attitude of gratitude seriously. Good job! Here's an exercise that can help you make your life even better. Start a journal and reflect on your days. You can easily include this in the habit of writing down three to five things you are grateful for. Take a couple of minutes at the end of your day just before going to sleep to take a look at what went well each day.

This exercise will help you get some perspective and focus on and relive the happy moments. Write everything down in your journal. This will give you an extra boost of happiness, motivation, and self-esteem every morning and evening.

The great thing is that just before going to sleep, you will be focusing on positive things, which will have a beneficial effect on your sleep and your subconscious mind. Why? Because your focus will be on the positive things of the day and gratitude instead of the negative things and things that didn't work well, which would probably keep you awake.

This is an extremely powerful exercise that has led to awesome changes in the lives of my clients and readers. But be careful. As always, focus on the positive. Focus on what went well. I'm saying this because many people look back at the day and judge it or remember everything that didn't go their way. They continuously relive situations and ask themselves what they could have or should have said, wonder who they could blame for what went wrong, or look for proof for how stuck they are or how bad things are going for them. *Don't do this.* This is just a waste of time that will keep you stuck!

You now know the enormous power of focus so here's what you do instead. Every night, before going to sleep, answer the following questions and in your journal:

- What am I grateful for (three to five points)?
- What three things made me happy today?
- What three things did I do particularly well today?
- How could I have made today even better?
- What is my most important goal for tomorrow?

As always, don't worry if the words don't start flowing right away when you do the exercise the first time. It's a matter of practice.

If you are blocked and can't think of anything, just stay with it for five minutes longer. Trust that the answers will come. Write the first things that come to mind without overthinking them or judging them. These things are often correct.

Don't worry about your style or mistakes. Just write! Do this every day for a month, and observe the changes that take place! A regular notebook or calendar will do.

Studies found out that journaling improves your focus, lowers stress, and has countless other health benefits. A study by the Department of Psychological Medicine, University of Auckland, New Zealand, from 2013 even found that journaling promotes faster wound healing! The members of the journaling group healed over 75% faster than their non-journaling counterparts.

Further research shows that journaling results in reduced absenteeism from work, quicker reemployment after a job loss, and higher GPAs for students. Think about it. People who wrote in their journal for as little as fifteen minutes a day healed their wounds faster, improved their immune systems, and improved their GPAs. If there were a pill for that, it would fly off the shelves!

Why am I always insisting so much on writing things down? Why can't you just have your goals and gratitude in your mind? Because writing about things puts them in perspective. By writing things down, you structure and organize your thoughts and feelings. As a result, you will sleep, feel, and think better. You'll even have a more vibrant social life. Almost certainly, your journaling will create momentum because you are reinforcing the positive over and over again.

It's your choice. This exercise can help you shift from seeing pain, negativity, and stress to looking at things through the lens of optimism, gratitude, hope, resilience, and purpose. You might not be able to change reality, but you can and should use your brain to change how you process the world around you, and that will change how you react to what happens to you.

It's time that you use the power of focus to change your reality. The journaling exercise will help you rewire your brain to see more of the positive things that exist around you.

And as I said before: If you are grateful for the things you have, more things to be grateful for will come into your life. It might even help you shift your inner dialogue from constant negative chatter to a more optimistic and positive outlook.

Another advantage of journaling is that you start to understand things better—most of all, yourself. You can find success patterns and discover how you can grow and learn from situations, which situations to avoid, how to react better, how to succeed faster next time, and which opportunities to seize. You will simply allow yourself to take inventory of all the positive moments of your day—the big ones and the small ones. Doing this every night you will build massive levels of confidence. Taking your life to the next level will become inevitable.

Action Step

1. Add the five new questions about into your gratitude journal. It's still just a five- to ten-minute exercise. It's a small price to pay for a life full of happiness, optimism, health, and faster wound healing.

CHAPTER TEN
Write a Thank-You Letter

I have another high impact exercise for you. If you want to do something genuinely magic that will improve your happiness and wellbeing even more, I recommend this little exercise. Write a thank-you letter. Science has found that it's not only hugely beneficial for the receiver but also for you, the sender.

Write a thank-you letter to the biggest influences in your life—the people who had a major positive impact on your life and who you never thanked. It could be your parents, teachers, coaches, friends, ex-bosses, colleagues, you name it!

Write to them saying what they did for you, how they influenced you, what they meant to you, and how they helped you. Take your time. It will be worth it! And while you are at it, why not write to one person a week?

Studies show that a gratitude letter can increase happiness and decrease depression for the person who writes it for as long as three months after the writing of the letter. It's said that the benefits are greatest if you deliver the message in person. Try writing a thank-you note, even if it's just a simple email.

Make showing gratitude to someone a daily habit. A colleague, the cashier in the supermarket, your parents, the mailman, your kids running or basketball coach—be creative. It's important to feel the gratitude and really think about the things you are thanking the person for. If it's trivial or not heartfelt, it doesn't work.

Scientists found out that writing a gratitude letter produces even more significant increases in happiness than the already powerful exercises I mentioned before, such as journaling and recalling past events you are grateful for. And there is more. They proved that writing multiple letters multiplies the effect of happiness and gratitude. Three out of four people who were part of this study wanted to keep writing gratitude letters even after the study was finished.

Why does writing work? Studies show that translating thoughts into words has advantages over just thinking thoughts. When we write, the thinking process is slowed down. Writing gives us the time to reflect on our thoughts because we think much faster than we write.

Everybody is hungry for genuine appreciation. Show people that they have mattered and do matter in your life. Show people that they are making the world a better place, and write them a thank-you letter, thank-you email, or thank-you note.

Action Steps

1. Sit down and make a list of five people who were a huge influence in your life or did something good for you.
2. Write a gratitude letter to each one of them.

CHAPTER ELEVEN
Gratitude sharpens your Focus

I know, I'm repeating myself. I've already mentioned it a couple of times, but the power of focus is so important and life-changing that it gets its own chapter.

Being grateful and feeling gratitude will train your power of focus. As a result of scanning your life for the good things in it—things to be grateful for, things to be happy about, and optimism—you will pick up more of the all the good things around you and feel better all the time. But it gets even better: The more your brain picks up on the positive, the more you'll expect this trend to continue, which results in being even more optimistic without even knowing if you are creating a self-fulfilling prophecy and an upward spiral.

Bad things happen, but it's what you choose to focus on that ultimately creates your reality. Victor Frankl, a Jewish psychologist who was imprisoned in a Germany concentration camp during the Second World War and who lost his entire family except for his sister, found that there is something good even in the worst circumstances. He became aware of what he called "the ultimate human freedom," which not even the Nazi prison wards could take away from him. They could control his external circumstances, but it was he who *chose* *how* these circumstances were going to affect him. Even if you're not able to control the circumstances that life presents to you, you can always choose your response to those circumstances and, by doing so, have a massive impact on your life.

Finding the positive doesn't mean being detached from the "real world" and ignoring the negative. Both can co-exist. That said, you have a huge power: the power of choice. You choose what enters your perception. The great thing is that once you expect positive outcomes, it's more possible for them to arise because our beliefs and expectations turn into self-fulfilling prophecies.

Your boss also will be happy. Why? What does your boss have to do with all this? Well, optimism is also one of the most powerful predictors of work performance. Optimists set more goals and put more effort into attaining these goals. They stay more committed in the face of difficulties and overcome obstacles more easily. They cope better with high-stress situations, and expecting positive outcomes makes it more possible for them to bounce back. There you go: win-win-win.

So with the gratitude exercises you learned in this book, which will take you around *five minutes* a day (max., ten), you are training your brain to become better at noticing and focusing on possibilities and opportunities for personal and professional growth and naturally getting better at seizing them and acting on them. But it gets even better. Your brain can only concentrate on so much at once because you have limited memory space, so what happens is that those little things that annoy you and the nagging negative voices at the back of your mind are pushed out.

Doing the gratitude exercises for just one week will make you happier and less depressed, and you'll see a significant difference after one, three, and six months. You'll even remain significantly happier and show higher levels of optimism after stopping the exercises. Still, I highly recommend you keep on doing the exercises because they will do miracles for you. You'll get better and better at scanning the world for good things and writing them down, and you'll see more and more opportunities wherever you look without even trying.

Make them a habit. Ritualize them. Do them at the same time each day. Keep what you need for doing these exercises easily available and convenient. For example, keep a journal on your nightstand. Clients of mine have told me that they had a lot of fun and got great results doing the exercises with children and spouses.

CHAPTER TWELVE
BONUS: The Power of Forgiveness

Having talked a lot about the massive power of gratitude, let's talk about another considerable force in our lives: the power of forgiveness.

Forgiveness is crucial on your way to success, fulfillment, and happiness. Sometimes, you can do everything right—you're following the habits of successful people, and you're doing your gratitude exercises every day—but you stay stuck. Nothing improves, and you don't know why. If this is happening, the chances are that there is some (energy) block because of a lack of forgiveness towards a person, situation, or even yourself (maybe you think you don't "deserve" good things like success or happiness).

I took a long, long time to learn this. Why on Earth should I forgive someone if that person did me wrong, and it's all their fault? The short answer: you're doing it for yourself, not for the other person. Forgiveness is not about being right or wrong. It's about you being well and not losing a ton of energy because anger and resentment—or worse, reliving hate over and over again—are huge energy drains. Do yourself a favor and let go!

A while ago I got an email from a reader. It read, "Although I've been doing the habits of your book regularly for months, I'm still stuck. I don't know what to do." Now. As a trained coach, I know I'm not supposed to give advice to a client but rather help the client come to her own conclusions by asking powerful questions. But I'm also a bestselling author of self-help books, and in that function, I can be more direct and even give advice, so I answered the following:

"Dear Jane,

Thank you for your e-mail. In my experience, if you do the habits and still don't move forward or are stuck there can only be two reasons:

1. You are nearly there. Resistance always gets bigger the closer you get to the goal. When you're close to giving up, you just have to push a little more.
   Solution: Hang in there a little bit longer.
2. You have a lack of gratitude or forgiveness. Sometimes, a lack of gratitude or forgiveness can block the flow on our way to success.
   Solution: Forgive everyone for everything."

I was not surprised to get the following answer: "Thank you for your answer, *but* I can't forgive them for what they did to me because …"

Yes, you can! You're not doing it for them; you're doing it for yourself. In 99.9% of cases, you not forgiving them has absolutely no impact on their lives but a significant impact on your life. As I mentioned before, *you* have the sleepless nights. *You* feel the bitterness. *You* are full of anger and don't enjoy the present moment. *You* are the one who is stuck due to the lack of forgiveness. *You* don't move forward. Yes, that's right, *you*, not them.

As outrageous as it sounds, send them love and forgiveness. Do it for selfish reasons. Know that you are doing it for *you*. Know that you're doing it to unblock *your* stuck energies. It's of no benefit at all to be angry at them. It will not change them, but you could get an ulcer from your anger, and that would actually benefit *them*.

Someone once said, "Holding a grudge against someone is like taking small doses of poison and hoping the other person will die from it."

As difficult as it seems, forgive and let go. Try it. The results might be mindboggling!

How? That's easy. First, make a list of everybody you are holding a grudge against. Second, make a list of everything you don't forgive yourself for. Third, work through the lists and forgive everything— even if it's super tricky. Search for a learning experience. Remember, you are doing it for you!

In the summer of 2017, I also got to taste a bit of my own medicine. In July of that year, *30 Days* was published by a major publisher in Japan. The forecasts were incredible. For weeks, my translator and editor were euphoric, predicting to sell 300,000 to 500,000 copies. I started to believe them. Once the book was in a thousand Japanese bookstores, it started happening. The first day was great! We were on point. The second day? Amazing! The Japanese can say after two days if a book will turn into a bestseller or not.

By the end of day two, I was already seeing my better half and me sipping piña coladas in a Caribbean tax paradise, but I also noted anger and grudges coming up. I noticed that I was starting to make a mental blacklist of people who had ignored me, rejected me, and made fun of me over the years on my way to the top (because that's where I thought I was going), and I planned to respond to them with a vengeance and the same disrespect. So that was my entertainment on day two.

And then day three came. It was a Saturday, and one of my toughest days in 2017. Suddenly, my Japanese contacts were not so optimistic anymore. All the euphoria was gone. The book stopped selling. I couldn't believe it. But we were doing so well! What happened?

First of all, I couldn't believe it, but my Japanese contacts convinced me that that's the way it works and that it would be a better idea to write another book because *30 Days* was dead. It won't sell anymore. No need for the planned reprints of thousands of copies.

An enormous sadness overcame me. Even worse, I was apathetic. The fall was long and hard. But after four hours of denial, self-pity, and wound-licking, I knew I needed to take a proactive approach.

I analyzed the situation and came to the conclusion that the problem was probably because of the grudges I had held and a shocking lack of forgiveness in my own life. So I started to make my lists. I spent the whole weekend forgiving.

While my Japanese contacts thought that the book was dead on Saturday and that there wouldn't be any reprints, news came suddenly on Tuesday.

"We're going to print another 5,000,." A week later, it was another 7,600. Two weeks later, by the end of July 2017, 25,600 copies were in print. Coincidence? I don' think so. I'm convinced that these additional 15,600 copies—although only a small fraction of the forecast—came from forgiving and letting go of grudges. And I'm still working on forgiveness because I still feel that my energy is not in full flow.

So if you are blocked or stuck in any way even though you are doing everything right, think about these two options:

1. Just hang in there a little longer.
2. Think about the grudges you're holding. Make your lists and start forgiving. At worst, you'll feel a lot lighter and happier. At best, the sky is the limit!

Let go, forgive the people who hurt you, forget them, and move on. But be careful. If you say "I forgive them, but I don't forget," you are not forgiving! This doesn't mean that you have to allow the people who hurt you to stay in your life or that you can't put limits on others' behavior or call them out on the spot. Forgiveness can be a mental exercise. They don't even have to know that they are forgiven. You simply need to understand the positive consequences and let go.

If you want to take it a little further, you can call up the people you have wronged or hurt and apologize. If that's too uncomfortable, write them a letter.

Above all, forgive yourself! When you learn to forgive yourself, it will be easier to forgive others. Just do it! The changes you will see when you manage to forgive others and, above all, yourself are amazing!

Forgive everybody who has wronged you (and most of all, yourself), and always remember Mahatma Gandhi, who said, "The weak can never forgive. Forgiveness is the attribute of the strong."

Action Steps

1. Make a list of everybody you haven't forgiven.
2. Make a list of everything you haven't forgiven yourself for.
3. Work on the lists.

Questions

1. What would your life be like if you accepted yourself just as you are without self-criticism?
2. What would your life be like if you forgave yourself and others?

CHAPTER THIRTEEN
What now?

Wow! That's it! I can't believe that we are already coming to the end of this book. It's the shortest book I have written so far but, surely, also one of the most powerful ones.

So that's it. I have given you seven powerful exercises. Do them, and your life will never be the same.

Don't give up if things don't go smoothly at first. It needs some time, but slowly, you'll get better and better at it thanks to the magic of discipline and repetition. If you need additional motivation, remember that science has proven that doing your gratitude exercises every day after four to six weeks *will* create amazing results. You should have five minutes a day to do these exercises no matter what your situation is. Tony Robbins once said, "If you don't have five minutes a day, you don't have a life."

A couple of years ago, I taught a semester of Happiness at the Geneva Business School in Barcelona. One of the homework assignments for the students was writing down three things they were grateful for every day. After some weeks, I saw precisely the benefits mentioned in this book when reading their assignments over the week: better sleep, better mood, more optimism, better social lives, and a lot more. This stuff really works.

You might be tempted to think that people are only grateful because they are happier, but it's actually the other way round. Gratitude has been proven to be a significant cause of positive outcomes and happiness.

I'll repeat it once more because it can't be said often enough: being grateful rewires your brain to see more of the positive things that are around you. You will see more opportunities, and you will see open doors for you where there wasn't even a door before.

Make gratitude a daily habit. When you are grateful for what you have, more things that you can be grateful for will come into your life. So be grateful for what you have and even for the things you don't have yet.

Sometimes, when you're going through a rough patch, it might be challenging to be grateful, I know. But believe me, there is always something to be grateful for, such as you, your body, your talents, your friends, your family, or nature. Start small. When I was jobless, I was grateful for drinking a coffee in the sun, having a good night's sleep, and having friends. Instead of starting your day by complaining about what you don't have or by dreading what is to come, start it by saying thank you for what you have. Focus on everything that's going well for you.

Stop comparing. Practice gratitude instead. Count your blessings instead of other people's blessings. This exercise alone can probably "cure" you of jealousy and envy if you practice it for three to four weeks.

The more I practice gratitude, the sweeter my day gets. I get up from my computer various times a day, go out, take a short five- to fifteen-minute walk, and feel gratitude. Feel the gratitude just after waking up and just before going to sleep. The first half an hour of your day sets the tone for the rest of your day. The last half an hour of your day is also critical. What you feed your brain in that time will keep vibrating during your sleep. It's these two times when your subconscious mind is the most active and most receptive.

Remember, your perception shapes your reality. Focusing on the positive can dramatically improve your success. This has been proven over and over again. Be patient, be consistent, and you will succeed.

Gratitude is not a magic pill, although it certainly has all the ingredients. Once you do the work in the real world, magic happens. I wish you this magic. All the best!

Marc

On the following pages <u>(starting on page 65)</u>, you have three months for journaling. *Start now*!

If you have bought the ebook versión you can download your 90-Day Gratitude Journal here

If you have bought the audiobook version contact me at marc@marcreklau.com and I'll send you the download link for the 90 Day Gratitude Journal

90 Day
Gratitude Journal

for

_____

Date:_____/_____/_____

Three things I'm grateful for:

_____

_____

_____

_____

Three things that I did particularly well today:

_____

_____

_____

_____

Three positive things that happened today:

_____

_____

_____

_____

How could I have made today even better?

_____

_____

_____

_____

What is my most important goal for tomorrow?

_____

_____

_____

_____

Date:_____/_____/_____

Three things I'm grateful for:

_____

_____

_____

_____

Three things that I did particularly well today:

_____

_____

_____

_____

Three positive things that happened today:

_____

_____

_____

_____

How could I have made today even better?

_____

_____

_____

_____

What is my most important goal for tomorrow?

_____

_____

_____

_____

Date:_____/_____/_____

Three things I'm grateful for:

_____

_____

_____

_____

Three things that I did particularly well today:

_____

_____

_____

_____

Three positive things that happened today:

_____

_____

_____

_____

How could I have made today even better?

_____

_____

_____

_____

What is my most important goal for tomorrow?

_____

_____

_____

_____

Date:_____/_____/_____

Three things I'm grateful for:

_____

_____

_____

_____

Three things that I did particularly well today:

_____

_____

_____

_____

Three positive things that happened today:

_____

_____

_____

_____

How could I have made today even better?

_____

_____

_____

_____

What is my most important goal for tomorrow?

_____

_____

_____

_____

Date:_____/_____/_____

Three things I'm grateful for:

_____

_____

_____

_____

Three things that I did particularly well today:

_____

_____

_____

_____

Three positive things that happened today:

_____

_____

_____

_____

How could I have made today even better?

_____

_____

_____

_____

What is my most important goal for tomorrow?

_____

_____

_____

_____

Date:_____/_____/_____

Three things I'm grateful for:

_____

_____

_____

_____

Three things that I did particularly well today:

_____

_____

_____

_____

Three positive things that happened today:

_____

_____

_____

_____

How could I have made today even better?

_____

_____

_____

_____

What is my most important goal for tomorrow?

_____

_____

_____

_____

Date:_____/_____/_____

Three things I'm grateful for:

_____

_____

_____

_____

Three things that I did particularly well today:

_____

_____

_____

_____

Three positive things that happened today:

_____

_____

_____

_____

How could I have made today even better?

_____

_____

_____

_____

What is my most important goal for tomorrow?

_____

_____

_____

_____

Date:_____/_____/_____

Three things I'm grateful for:

_____
_____
_____
_____

Three things that I did particularly well today:

_____
_____
_____
_____

Three positive things that happened today:

_____
_____
_____
_____

How could I have made today even better?

_____
_____
_____
_____

What is my most important goal for tomorrow?

_____
_____
_____
_____

Date:_____/_____/_____

Three things I'm grateful for:

_____

_____

_____

_____

Three things that I did particularly well today:

_____

_____

_____

_____

Three positive things that happened today:

_____

_____

_____

_____

How could I have made today even better?

_____

_____

_____

_____

What is my most important goal for tomorrow?

_____

_____

_____

_____

Date:_____/_____/_____

Three things I'm grateful for:

_____
_____
_____
_____

Three things that I did particularly well today:

_____
_____
_____
_____

Three positive things that happened today:

_____
_____
_____
_____

How could I have made today even better?

_____
_____
_____
_____

What is my most important goal for tomorrow?

_____
_____
_____
_____

Date:_____/_____/_____

Three things I'm grateful for:

_____

_____

_____

_____

Three things that I did particularly well today:

_____

_____

_____

_____

Three positive things that happened today:

_____

_____

_____

_____

How could I have made today even better?

_____

_____

_____

_____

What is my most important goal for tomorrow?

_____

_____

_____

_____

Date:_____/_____/_____

Three things I'm grateful for:

_____

_____

_____

_____

Three things that I did particularly well today:

_____

_____

_____

_____

Three positive things that happened today:

_____

_____

_____

_____

How could I have made today even better?

_____

_____

_____

_____

What is my most important goal for tomorrow?

_____

_____

_____

_____

Date:_____/_____/_____

Three things I'm grateful for:

_____
_____
_____
_____

Three things that I did particularly well today:

_____
_____
_____
_____

Three positive things that happened today:

_____
_____
_____
_____

How could I have made today even better?

_____
_____
_____
_____

What is my most important goal for tomorrow?

_____
_____
_____
_____

Date:_____/_____/_____

Three things I'm grateful for:

_____

_____

_____

_____

Three things that I did particularly well today:

_____

_____

_____

_____

Three positive things that happened today:

_____

_____

_____

_____

How could I have made today even better?

_____

_____

_____

_____

What is my most important goal for tomorrow?

_____

_____

_____

_____

Date:_____/_____/_____

Three things I'm grateful for:

_____
_____
_____
_____

Three things that I did particularly well today:

_____
_____
_____
_____

Three positive things that happened today:

_____
_____
_____
_____

How could I have made today even better?

_____
_____
_____
_____

What is my most important goal for tomorrow?

_____
_____
_____
_____

Date:_____/_____/_____

Three things I'm grateful for:

_____

_____

_____

_____

Three things that I did particularly well today:

_____

_____

_____

_____

Three positive things that happened today:

_____

_____

_____

_____

How could I have made today even better?

_____

_____

_____

_____

What is my most important goal for tomorrow?

_____

_____

_____

_____

Date:_____/_____/_____

Three things I'm grateful for:

_____

_____

_____

_____

Three things that I did particularly well today:

_____

_____

_____

_____

Three positive things that happened today:

_____

_____

_____

_____

How could I have made today even better?

_____

_____

_____

_____

What is my most important goal for tomorrow?

_____

_____

_____

_____

Date:_____/_____/_____

Three things I'm grateful for:

_____
_____
_____
_____

Three things that I did particularly well today:

_____
_____
_____
_____

Three positive things that happened today:

_____
_____
_____
_____

How could I have made today even better?

_____
_____
_____
_____

What is my most important goal for tomorrow?

_____
_____
_____
_____

Date:_____/_____/_____

Three things I'm grateful for:

_____

_____

_____

_____

Three things that I did particularly well today:

_____

_____

_____

_____

Three positive things that happened today:

_____

_____

_____

_____

How could I have made today even better?

_____

_____

_____

_____

What is my most important goal for tomorrow?

_____

_____

_____

_____

Date:_____/_____/_____

Three things I'm grateful for:

_____

_____

_____

_____

Three things that I did particularly well today:

_____

_____

_____

_____

Three positive things that happened today:

_____

_____

_____

_____

How could I have made today even better?

_____

_____

_____

_____

What is my most important goal for tomorrow?

_____

_____

_____

_____

Date:_____/_____/_____

Three things I'm grateful for:

_____
_____
_____
_____

Three things that I did particularly well today:

_____
_____
_____
_____

Three positive things that happened today:

_____
_____
_____
_____

How could I have made today even better?

_____
_____
_____
_____

What is my most important goal for tomorrow?

_____
_____
_____
_____

Date:_____/_____/_____

Three things I'm grateful for:

_____

_____

_____

_____

Three things that I did particularly well today:

_____

_____

_____

_____

Three positive things that happened today:

_____

_____

_____

_____

How could I have made today even better?

_____

_____

_____

_____

What is my most important goal for tomorrow?

_____

_____

_____

_____

Date:_____/_____/_____

Three things I'm grateful for:

_____
_____
_____
_____

Three things that I did particularly well today:

_____
_____
_____
_____

Three positive things that happened today:

_____
_____
_____
_____

How could I have made today even better?

_____
_____
_____
_____

What is my most important goal for tomorrow?

_____
_____
_____
_____

Date:_____/_____/_____

Three things I'm grateful for:

_____
_____
_____
_____

Three things that I did particularly well today:

_____
_____
_____
_____

Three positive things that happened today:

_____
_____
_____
_____

How could I have made today even better?

_____
_____
_____
_____

What is my most important goal for tomorrow?

_____
_____
_____
_____

Date:_____/_____/_____

Three things I'm grateful for:

_____
_____
_____
_____

Three things that I did particularly well today:

_____
_____
_____
_____

Three positive things that happened today:

_____
_____
_____
_____

How could I have made today even better?

_____
_____
_____
_____

What is my most important goal for tomorrow?

_____
_____
_____
_____

Date:_____/_____/_____

Three things I'm grateful for:

_____

_____

_____

_____

Three things that I did particularly well today:

_____

_____

_____

_____

Three positive things that happened today:

_____

_____

_____

_____

How could I have made today even better?

_____

_____

_____

_____

What is my most important goal for tomorrow?

_____

_____

_____

_____

Date:_____/_____/_____

Three things I'm grateful for:

_____

_____

_____

_____

Three things that I did particularly well today:

_____

_____

_____

_____

Three positive things that happened today:

_____

_____

_____

_____

How could I have made today even better?

_____

_____

_____

_____

What is my most important goal for tomorrow?

_____

_____

_____

_____

Date:_____/_____/_____

Three things I'm grateful for:

_____
_____
_____
_____

Three things that I did particularly well today:

_____
_____
_____
_____

Three positive things that happened today:

_____
_____
_____
_____

How could I have made today even better?

_____
_____
_____
_____

What is my most important goal for tomorrow?

_____
_____
_____
_____

Date:_____/_____/_____

Three things I'm grateful for:

_____
_____
_____
_____

Three things that I did particularly well today:

_____
_____
_____
_____

Three positive things that happened today:

_____
_____
_____
_____

How could I have made today even better?

_____
_____
_____
_____

What is my most important goal for tomorrow?

_____
_____
_____
_____

Date:_____/_____/_____

Three things I'm grateful for:

_____
_____
_____
_____

Three things that I did particularly well today:

_____
_____
_____
_____

Three positive things that happened today:

_____
_____
_____
_____

How could I have made today even better?

_____
_____
_____
_____

What is my most important goal for tomorrow?

_____
_____
_____
_____

Date:_____/_____/_____

Three things I'm grateful for:

_____

_____

_____

_____

Three things that I did particularly well today:

_____

_____

_____

_____

Three positive things that happened today:

_____

_____

_____

_____

How could I have made today even better?

_____

_____

_____

_____

What is my most important goal for tomorrow?

_____

_____

_____

_____

Date:_____/_____/_____

Three things I'm grateful for:

_____
_____
_____
_____

Three things that I did particularly well today:

_____
_____
_____
_____

Three positive things that happened today:

_____
_____
_____
_____

How could I have made today even better?

_____
_____
_____
_____

What is my most important goal for tomorrow?

_____
_____
_____
_____

Date:_____/_____/_____

Three things I'm grateful for:

_____

_____

_____

_____

Three things that I did particularly well today:

_____

_____

_____

_____

Three positive things that happened today:

_____

_____

_____

_____

How could I have made today even better?

_____

_____

_____

_____

What is my most important goal for tomorrow?

_____

_____

_____

_____

Date:_____/_____/_____

Three things I'm grateful for:

_____
_____
_____
_____

Three things that I did particularly well today:

_____
_____
_____
_____

Three positive things that happened today:

_____
_____
_____
_____

How could I have made today even better?

_____
_____
_____
_____

What is my most important goal for tomorrow?

_____
_____
_____
_____

Date:_____/_____/_____

Three things I'm grateful for:

_____
_____
_____
_____

Three things that I did particularly well today:

_____
_____
_____
_____

Three positive things that happened today:

_____
_____
_____
_____

How could I have made today even better?

_____
_____
_____
_____

What is my most important goal for tomorrow?

_____
_____
_____
_____

Date:_____ / _____ / _____

Three things I'm grateful for:

_____

_____

_____

_____

Three things that I did particularly well today:

_____

_____

_____

_____

Three positive things that happened today:

_____

_____

_____

_____

How could I have made today even better?

_____

_____

_____

_____

What is my most important goal for tomorrow?

_____

_____

_____

_____

Date:_____/_____/_____

Three things I'm grateful for:

_____
_____
_____
_____

Three things that I did particularly well today:

_____
_____
_____
_____

Three positive things that happened today:

_____
_____
_____
_____

How could I have made today even better?

_____
_____
_____
_____

What is my most important goal for tomorrow?

_____
_____
_____
_____

Date:_____/_____/_____

Three things I'm grateful for:

_____

_____

_____

_____

Three things that I did particularly well today:

_____

_____

_____

_____

Three positive things that happened today:

_____

_____

_____

_____

How could I have made today even better?

_____

_____

_____

_____

What is my most important goal for tomorrow?

_____

_____

_____

_____

Date:_____/_____/_____

Three things I'm grateful for:

_____

_____

_____

_____

Three things that I did particularly well today:

_____

_____

_____

_____

Three positive things that happened today:

_____

_____

_____

_____

How could I have made today even better?

_____

_____

_____

_____

What is my most important goal for tomorrow?

_____

_____

_____

_____

Date:_____/_____/_____

Three things I'm grateful for:

_____

_____

_____

_____

Three things that I did particularly well today:

_____

_____

_____

_____

Three positive things that happened today:

_____

_____

_____

_____

How could I have made today even better?

_____

_____

_____

_____

What is my most important goal for tomorrow?

_____

_____

_____

_____

Date:_____/_____/_____

Three things I'm grateful for:

_____

_____

_____

_____

Three things that I did particularly well today:

_____

_____

_____

_____

Three positive things that happened today:

_____

_____

_____

_____

How could I have made today even better?

_____

_____

_____

_____

What is my most important goal for tomorrow?

_____

_____

_____

_____

Date:_____/_____/_____

Three things I'm grateful for:

_____

_____

_____

_____

Three things that I did particularly well today:

_____

_____

_____

_____

Three positive things that happened today:

_____

_____

_____

_____

How could I have made today even better?

_____

_____

_____

_____

What is my most important goal for tomorrow?

_____

_____

_____

_____

Date:_____/_____/_____

Three things I'm grateful for:

_____
_____
_____
_____

Three things that I did particularly well today:

_____
_____
_____
_____

Three positive things that happened today:

_____
_____
_____
_____

How could I have made today even better?

_____
_____
_____
_____

What is my most important goal for tomorrow?

_____
_____
_____
_____

Date:_____/_____/_____

Three things I'm grateful for:

_____

_____

_____

_____

Three things that I did particularly well today:

_____

_____

_____

_____

Three positive things that happened today:

_____

_____

_____

_____

How could I have made today even better?

_____

_____

_____

_____

What is my most important goal for tomorrow?

_____

_____

_____

_____

Date:_____/_____/_____

Three things I'm grateful for:

_____

_____

_____

_____

Three things that I did particularly well today:

_____

_____

_____

_____

Three positive things that happened today:

_____

_____

_____

_____

How could I have made today even better?

_____

_____

_____

_____

What is my most important goal for tomorrow?

_____

_____

_____

_____

Date:_____/_____/_____

Three things I'm grateful for:

_____

_____

_____

_____

Three things that I did particularly well today:

_____

_____

_____

_____

Three positive things that happened today:

_____

_____

_____

_____

How could I have made today even better?

_____

_____

_____

_____

What is my most important goal for tomorrow?

_____

_____

_____

_____

Date:_____/_____/_____

Three things I'm grateful for:

_____
_____
_____
_____

Three things that I did particularly well today:

_____
_____
_____
_____

Three positive things that happened today:

_____
_____
_____
_____

How could I have made today even better?

_____
_____
_____
_____

What is my most important goal for tomorrow?

_____
_____
_____
_____

Date:_____/_____/_____

Three things I'm grateful for:

_____

_____

_____

_____

Three things that I did particularly well today:

_____

_____

_____

_____

Three positive things that happened today:

_____

_____

_____

_____

How could I have made today even better?

_____

_____

_____

_____

What is my most important goal for tomorrow?

_____

_____

_____

_____

Date:_____/_____/_____

Three things I'm grateful for:

_____

_____

_____

_____

Three things that I did particularly well today:

_____

_____

_____

_____

Three positive things that happened today:

_____

_____

_____

_____

How could I have made today even better?

_____

_____

_____

_____

What is my most important goal for tomorrow?

_____

_____

_____

_____

Date:_____/_____/_____

Three things I'm grateful for:

_____

_____

_____

_____

Three things that I did particularly well today:

_____

_____

_____

_____

Three positive things that happened today:

_____

_____

_____

_____

How could I have made today even better?

_____

_____

_____

_____

What is my most important goal for tomorrow?

_____

_____

_____

_____

Date:_____/_____/_____

Three things I'm grateful for:

_____

_____

_____

_____

Three things that I did particularly well today:

_____

_____

_____

_____

Three positive things that happened today:

_____

_____

_____

_____

How could I have made today even better?

_____

_____

_____

_____

What is my most important goal for tomorrow?

_____

_____

_____

_____

Date:_____/_____/_____

Three things I'm grateful for:

_____

_____

_____

_____

Three things that I did particularly well today:

_____

_____

_____

_____

Three positive things that happened today:

_____

_____

_____

_____

How could I have made today even better?

_____

_____

_____

_____

What is my most important goal for tomorrow?

_____

_____

_____

_____

Date:_____/_____/_____

Three things I'm grateful for:

_____

_____

_____

_____

Three things that I did particularly well today:

_____

_____

_____

_____

Three positive things that happened today:

_____

_____

_____

_____

How could I have made today even better?

_____

_____

_____

_____

What is my most important goal for tomorrow?

_____

_____

_____

_____

Date:_____/_____/_____

Three things I'm grateful for:

_____
_____
_____
_____

Three things that I did particularly well today:

_____
_____
_____
_____

Three positive things that happened today:

_____
_____
_____
_____

How could I have made today even better?

_____
_____
_____
_____

What is my most important goal for tomorrow?

_____
_____
_____
_____

Date:_____/_____/_____

Three things I'm grateful for:

_____

_____

_____

_____

Three things that I did particularly well today:

_____

_____

_____

_____

Three positive things that happened today:

_____

_____

_____

_____

How could I have made today even better?

_____

_____

_____

_____

What is my most important goal for tomorrow?

_____

_____

_____

_____

Date:_____/_____/_____

Three things I'm grateful for:

_____

_____

_____

_____

Three things that I did particularly well today:

_____

_____

_____

_____

Three positive things that happened today:

_____

_____

_____

_____

How could I have made today even better?

_____

_____

_____

_____

What is my most important goal for tomorrow?

_____

_____

_____

_____

Date:_____/_____/_____

Three things I'm grateful for:

_____

_____

_____

_____

Three things that I did particularly well today:

_____

_____

_____

_____

Three positive things that happened today:

_____

_____

_____

_____

How could I have made today even better?

_____

_____

_____

_____

What is my most important goal for tomorrow?

_____

_____

_____

_____

Date:_____/_____/_____

Three things I'm grateful for:

_____
_____
_____
_____

Three things that I did particularly well today:

_____
_____
_____
_____

Three positive things that happened today:

_____
_____
_____
_____

How could I have made today even better?

_____
_____
_____
_____

What is my most important goal for tomorrow?

_____
_____
_____
_____

Date:_____/_____/_____

Three things I'm grateful for:

_____
_____
_____
_____

Three things that I did particularly well today:

_____
_____
_____
_____

Three positive things that happened today:

_____
_____
_____
_____

How could I have made today even better?

_____
_____
_____
_____

What is my most important goal for tomorrow?

_____
_____
_____
_____

Date:_____/_____/_____

Three things I'm grateful for:

_____
_____
_____
_____

Three things that I did particularly well today:

_____
_____
_____
_____

Three positive things that happened today:

_____
_____
_____
_____

How could I have made today even better?

_____
_____
_____
_____

What is my most important goal for tomorrow?

_____
_____
_____
_____

Date:_____/_____/_____

Three things I'm grateful for:

_____

_____

_____

_____

Three things that I did particularly well today:

_____

_____

_____

_____

Three positive things that happened today:

_____

_____

_____

_____

How could I have made today even better?

_____

_____

_____

_____

What is my most important goal for tomorrow?

_____

_____

_____

_____

Date:_____/_____/_____

Three things I'm grateful for:

_____

_____

_____

_____

Three things that I did particularly well today:

_____

_____

_____

_____

Three positive things that happened today:

_____

_____

_____

_____

How could I have made today even better?

_____

_____

_____

_____

What is my most important goal for tomorrow?

_____

_____

_____

_____

Date:_____/_____/_____

Three things I'm grateful for:

_____
_____
_____
_____

Three things that I did particularly well today:

_____
_____
_____
_____

Three positive things that happened today:

_____
_____
_____
_____

How could I have made today even better?

_____
_____
_____
_____

What is my most important goal for tomorrow?

_____
_____
_____
_____

Date:_____/_____/_____

Three things I'm grateful for:

_____

_____

_____

_____

Three things that I did particularly well today:

_____

_____

_____

_____

Three positive things that happened today:

_____

_____

_____

_____

How could I have made today even better?

_____

_____

_____

_____

What is my most important goal for tomorrow?

_____

_____

_____

_____

Date:_____/_____/_____

Three things I'm grateful for:

_____
_____
_____
_____

Three things that I did particularly well today:

_____
_____
_____
_____

Three positive things that happened today:

_____
_____
_____
_____

How could I have made today even better?

_____
_____
_____
_____

What is my most important goal for tomorrow?

_____
_____
_____
_____

Date:_____/_____/_____

Three things I'm grateful for:

_____
_____
_____
_____

Three things that I did particularly well today:

_____
_____
_____
_____

Three positive things that happened today:

_____
_____
_____
_____

How could I have made today even better?

_____
_____
_____
_____

What is my most important goal for tomorrow?

_____
_____
_____
_____

Date:_____/_____/_____

Three things I'm grateful for:

_____
_____
_____
_____

Three things that I did particularly well today:

_____
_____
_____
_____

Three positive things that happened today:

_____
_____
_____
_____

How could I have made today even better?

_____
_____
_____
_____

What is my most important goal for tomorrow?

_____
_____
_____
_____

Date:_____/_____/_____

Three things I'm grateful for:

_____

_____

_____

_____

Three things that I did particularly well today:

_____

_____

_____

_____

Three positive things that happened today:

_____

_____

_____

_____

How could I have made today even better?

_____

_____

_____

_____

What is my most important goal for tomorrow?

_____

_____

_____

_____

Date:_____/_____/_____

Three things I'm grateful for:

_____
_____
_____
_____

Three things that I did particularly well today:

_____
_____
_____
_____

Three positive things that happened today:

_____
_____
_____
_____

How could I have made today even better?

_____
_____
_____
_____

What is my most important goal for tomorrow?

_____
_____
_____
_____

Date:_____/_____/_____

Three things I'm grateful for:

_____

_____

_____

_____

Three things that I did particularly well today:

_____

_____

_____

_____

Three positive things that happened today:

_____

_____

_____

_____

How could I have made today even better?

_____

_____

_____

_____

What is my most important goal for tomorrow?

_____

_____

_____

_____

Date:_____/_____/_____

Three things I'm grateful for:

_____
_____
_____
_____

Three things that I did particularly well today:

_____
_____
_____
_____

Three positive things that happened today:

_____
_____
_____
_____

How could I have made today even better?

_____
_____
_____
_____

What is my most important goal for tomorrow?

_____
_____
_____
_____

Date:_____/_____/_____

Three things I'm grateful for:

_____
_____
_____
_____

Three things that I did particularly well today:

_____
_____
_____
_____

Three positive things that happened today:

_____
_____
_____
_____

How could I have made today even better?

_____
_____
_____
_____

What is my most important goal for tomorrow?

_____
_____
_____
_____

Date:_____/_____/_____

Three things I'm grateful for:

_____
_____
_____
_____

Three things that I did particularly well today:

_____
_____
_____
_____

Three positive things that happened today:

_____
_____
_____
_____

How could I have made today even better?

_____
_____
_____
_____

What is my most important goal for tomorrow?

_____
_____
_____
_____

Date:_____/_____/_____

Three things I'm grateful for:

_____

_____

_____

_____

Three things that I did particularly well today:

_____

_____

_____

_____

Three positive things that happened today:

_____

_____

_____

_____

How could I have made today even better?

_____

_____

_____

_____

What is my most important goal for tomorrow?

_____

_____

_____

_____

Date:_____/_____/_____

Three things I'm grateful for:

_____

_____

_____

_____

Three things that I did particularly well today:

_____

_____

_____

_____

Three positive things that happened today:

_____

_____

_____

_____

How could I have made today even better?

_____

_____

_____

_____

What is my most important goal for tomorrow?

_____

_____

_____

_____

Date:_____/_____/_____

Three things I'm grateful for:

_____

_____

_____

_____

Three things that I did particularly well today:

_____

_____

_____

_____

Three positive things that happened today:

_____

_____

_____

_____

How could I have made today even better?

_____

_____

_____

What is my most important goal for tomorrow?

_____

_____

_____

_____

Date:_____/_____/_____

Three things I'm grateful for:

_____
_____
_____
_____

Three things that I did particularly well today:

_____
_____
_____
_____

Three positive things that happened today:

_____
_____
_____
_____

How could I have made today even better?

_____
_____
_____
_____

What is my most important goal for tomorrow?

_____
_____
_____
_____

Date:_____/_____/_____

Three things I'm grateful for:

_____

_____

_____

_____

Three things that I did particularly well today:

_____

_____

_____

_____

Three positive things that happened today:

_____

_____

_____

_____

How could I have made today even better?

_____

_____

_____

_____

What is my most important goal for tomorrow?

_____

_____

_____

_____

Date:_____/_____/_____

Three things I'm grateful for:

_____
_____
_____
_____

Three things that I did particularly well today:

_____
_____
_____
_____

Three positive things that happened today:

_____
_____
_____
_____

How could I have made today even better?

_____
_____
_____
_____

What is my most important goal for tomorrow?

_____
_____
_____
_____

Date:_____/_____/_____

Three things I'm grateful for:

_____

_____

_____

_____

Three things that I did particularly well today:

_____

_____

_____

_____

Three positive things that happened today:

_____

_____

_____

_____

How could I have made today even better?

_____

_____

_____

_____

What is my most important goal for tomorrow?

_____

_____

_____

_____

Date:_____/_____/_____

Three things I'm grateful for:

_____
_____
_____
_____

Three things that I did particularly well today:

_____
_____
_____
_____

Three positive things that happened today:

_____
_____
_____
_____

How could I have made today even better?

_____
_____
_____
_____

What is my most important goal for tomorrow?

_____
_____
_____
_____

Date:_____/_____/_____

Three things I'm grateful for:

_____

_____

_____

_____

Three things that I did particularly well today:

_____

_____

_____

_____

Three positive things that happened today:

_____

_____

_____

_____

How could I have made today even better?

_____

_____

_____

_____

What is my most important goal for tomorrow?

_____

_____

_____

_____

Date:_____/_____/_____

Three things I'm grateful for:

_____

_____

_____

_____

Three things that I did particularly well today:

_____

_____

_____

_____

Three positive things that happened today:

_____

_____

_____

_____

How could I have made today even better?

_____

_____

_____

_____

What is my most important goal for tomorrow?

_____

_____

_____

_____

Date:_____/_____/_____

Three things I'm grateful for:

_____
_____
_____
_____

Three things that I did particularly well today:

_____
_____
_____
_____

Three positive things that happened today:

_____
_____
_____
_____

How could I have made today even better?

_____
_____
_____
_____

What is my most important goal for tomorrow?

_____
_____
_____
_____

Date:_____/_____/_____

Three things I'm grateful for:

_____

_____

_____

_____

Three things that I did particularly well today:

_____

_____

_____

_____

Three positive things that happened today:

_____

_____

_____

_____

How could I have made today even better?

_____

_____

_____

_____

What is my most important goal for tomorrow?

_____

_____

_____

_____

Date:_____/_____/_____

Three things I'm grateful for:

_____

_____

_____

_____

Three things that I did particularly well today:

_____

_____

_____

_____

Three positive things that happened today:

_____

_____

_____

_____

How could I have made today even better?

_____

_____

_____

_____

What is my most important goal for tomorrow?

_____

_____

_____

_____

Date:_____/_____/_____

Three things I'm grateful for:

_____
_____
_____
_____

Three things that I did particularly well today:

_____
_____
_____
_____

Three positive things that happened today:

_____
_____
_____
_____

How could I have made today even better?

_____
_____
_____
_____

What is my most important goal for tomorrow?

_____
_____
_____
_____

Date:_____/_____/_____

Three things I'm grateful for:

_____
_____
_____
_____

Three things that I did particularly well today:

_____
_____
_____
_____

Three positive things that happened today:

_____
_____
_____
_____

How could I have made today even better?

_____
_____
_____
_____

What is my most important goal for tomorrow?

_____
_____
_____
_____

Date:_____/_____/_____

Three things I'm grateful for:

_____
_____
_____
_____

Three things that I did particularly well today:

_____
_____
_____
_____

Three positive things that happened today:

_____
_____
_____
_____

How could I have made today even better?

_____
_____
_____
_____

What is my most important goal for tomorrow?

_____
_____
_____
_____

Date:_____/_____/_____

Three things I'm grateful for:

_____
_____
_____
_____

Three things that I did particularly well today:

_____
_____
_____
_____

Three positive things that happened today:

_____
_____
_____
_____

How could I have made today even better?

_____
_____
_____
_____

What is my most important goal for tomorrow?

_____
_____
_____
_____

I Need Your Help

Thank You Very Much For Downloading or Buying My Book!

I really appreciate your feedback, and love hearing what you have to say.

Your input is important for me to make my next book(s) even better.

If you liked the book please be so kind and leave an honest review on Amazon! It really helps other people to find the book!
Five stars would be great though ;-)

Thank you so much!! Marc

One last thing...

If you have been inspired by this book and want to help others to reach their goals and improve their lives, here are some action steps you can take immediately to make a positive difference:

- Gift it to friends, family, colleagues and even strangers so that they can also learn that they con reach their goals and live great lives.

- Please share your thoughts about this book on Twitter, Facebook and Instagram or write a book review. It helps other people to find it.

- If you own a business or if you are a manager - or even if you're not - gift some copies to your team or employees and improve the productivity of your company.
Contact me at marc@marcreklau.com. I'll give you a 30% discount on bulk orders.

- If you have a Podcast or know somebody that has one ask them to interview me. I'm always happy to spread the message of 30 DAYS and help people improve their lives. You can also ask you local newspaper, radio station, or online media outlets to interview me :)

Bring the simple steps of 30 DAYS to your Organization

Help each member of your organization to succeed. My bestselling book *30 DAYS - change your habits change your life* is available at a special price on bulk orders for businesses, universities, schools, governments, NGOs, and community groups.

It's the ideal gift to inspire your friends, colleagues and team members to reach their fullest potential and make real, sustainable changes.

Contact marc@marcreklau.com

To book a presentation based on 30 DAYS or my book Destination Happiness contact me with an e-mail to marc@marcreklau.com

About the Author

Marc Reklau is a Coach, Speaker, and author of 9 books including the international #1 Bestseller *"30 Days - Change your habits, change your life"*, which since April 2015 has been sold and downloaded over 180,000 times and has been translated into Spanish, German, Japanese, Chinese, Russian, Thai, Indonesian, Portuguese and Korean among others.

He wrote the book in 2014 after being fired from his job and literally went from jobless to Bestseller (which is actually the title of his second book).

The Spanish version of his book "Destination Happiness" has been published by Spain's #1 Publisher Planeta in January 2018.

Marc's mission is to empower people to create the life they want and to give them the resources and tools to make it happen.

His message is simple: Many people want to change things in their lives, but few are willing to do a simple set of exercises constantly over a period of time. You can plan and create success and happiness in your life by installing habits that support you on the way to your goals.

If you want to work with Marc directly contact him on his homepage www.marcreklau.com where you also find more information about him.

You can connect with him on Twitter @MarcReklau, Facebook or on his website www.goodhabitsacademy.com

You may also like:

30 Days - Change your habits, change your life
Contains the best strategies to help you to create the life you want.
The book is based on science, neuroscience, positive psychology and
real-life examples and contains the best exercises to quickly create
momentum towards a happier, healthier and wealthier life.
Thirty days can really make a difference if you do things consistently
and develop new habits!

More than 180,000 combined sales and downloads since March 2015.

From Jobless to Amazon Bestseller
From Jobless to Amazon Bestseller shows you the simple, step-by-
step system that author Marc Reklau used to write, self publish,
market and promote his books to over 200,000 combined sales and
downloads on Amazon.

The Productivity Revolution
What if you could dramatically increase your productivity? What if
you could stop being overwhelmed and get an extra hour a day to do
the things you love? What would finally having time to spend with
your family, some alone time to read, or exercise mean to you?
Learn the best strategies to double your productivity and get things
done in this book.

More than 10,000 copies sold!

Destination Happiness
In Destination Happiness bestselling author, Marc Reklau, shows you
scientifically proven exercises and habits that help you to achieve a
successful, meaningful and happy life. Science has proven that
Happiness and Optimism can be learned. Learn the best and
scientifically proven methods to improve your life now and don't be
fooled by the simplicity of some of the exercises!

Love Yourself First!

Having healthy self-esteem is being happy with ourselves and believing that we deserve to enjoy the good things in life, exactly like every other person on this planet. Our self-esteem impacts every area of our life: our self-confidence, our relationships with other, the partner or job we choose, our happiness, our inner peace and even our personal and professional success. This book shows you in a very simple and fun way how to raise your self-esteem by doing some of the little exercises it presents to you.

How to become a people Magnet

"How to become a People Magnet" reveals the secrets and psychology behind successful relationships with other people. Your success and happiness in life - at home and in business -, to a great extent, depend on how you get along with other people. **The most successful people**, quite often, aren't the ones with superior intelligence or the best skills, and the happiest people most times aren't smarter than we are, yet they **are the ones who have the greatest people skills.**

Sold over 1300 copies in the month of its launch.

Made in the USA
Las Vegas, NV
14 February 2024

85804147R00100